MW00966369

THE ROYAL HORTICULTURAL SOCIETY
ADDRESS BOOK

Commentary by Brent Elliott

Illustrations from the
Royal Horticultural Society's Lindley Library

FRANCES LINCOLN

Frances Lincoln Limited
4 Torriano Mews
Torriano Avenue
London NW5 2RZ
www.franceslincoln.com

The Royal Horticultural Society Address Book
Copyright © Frances Lincoln Limited 2003

Text and illustrations copyright © the Royal Horticultural Society 2003
and printed under licence granted by the Royal Horticultural Society,
Registered Charity number 222879. Profits from the sale of this address book
are an important contribution to the funds raised by the Royal Horticultural Society.
For more information visit our website or call 0845 130 4646.

An interest in gardening is all you need to enjoy being a member of the RHS.

Website: www.rhs.org.uk

British Library cataloguing-in-publication data
A catalogue record for this book is available from the British Library

ISBN 0-7112-2091-3

Printed in China
First Frances Lincoln edition 2003

FRONT COVER
A late nineteenth-century drawing of *Clematis × jackmanii*
by Ruth Glaister. Gift of Mrs Agnes Elmhurst, 1954.

BACK COVER
An early nineteenth-century drawing of the star anemone (*Anemone pavonina*) by Pierre-Jean-François Turpin,
from an album of his drawings on vellum. Reginald Cory bequest, 1936.

TITLE PAGE
An early nineteenth-century drawing of a ranunculus by Pierre-Jean-François Turpin,
from an album of his drawings on vellum. Reginald Cory bequest, 1936.

OVERLEAF, RIGHT
A late nineteenth-century drawing of the oriental poppy (*Papaver orientale*)
by Ruth Glaister. Gift of Mrs Agnes Elmhurst, 1954.

ntroduction

1859, on the verge of bankruptcy, the Horticultural Society of London sold its original library. e sale took three days at Sotheby's, thousands of books and drawings were parcelled out in lots, the total profit to the Society was £1,112 1s. 6d.

Seven years later, when the re-named Royal Horticultural Society was once again flourishing, the vate library of its former Secretary, John Lindley, came on the market. Using the profits from the st International Horticultural Exhibition, which it had just helped to stage, the RHS bought dley's collection as a partial replacement for the library it had lost. In 1868 the collection was ested in a private trust, the Lindley Library Trust, in order to ensure that it could never again be d as its predecessor had been. Today, the Lindley Library is a collective term for all the books, riodicals and drawings owned by the Royal Horticultural Society, and occupies five sites, from rlow Carr in the north to Hyde Hall in the east to Wisley in the south. The largest collection, ich also includes the historical collection, is housed in London at 80 Vincent Square.

John Lindley's library comprised some 1,300 volumes. Today, the collection in London alone ludes roughly 50,000 volumes, 1,500 periodical titles (about 400 of these are current publications eived as gifts or exchanges), trade catalogues from some 7,000 firms worldwide and 28,000 wings. The collections have been built up by purchase, commission, gifts, exchanges and bequests, d the illustrations in this address book have been chosen to show the range of gifts and bequests eived by the Lindley Library over the years.

By far the largest single bequest was that of Reginald Cory (1871–1934), a Cardiff coal millionaire o inherited a fine house and garden at the Dyffryn, near Cardiff. Cory lavished his wealth on books d drawings and enthusiastically promoted horticultural causes, from dahlia trials to helping to ance the ailing *Curtis's Botanical Magazine*. His bequest of books and drawings was received in 1936 d returned to the Library some of the very items sold at Sotheby's in 1859.

There have been many other bequests: artists have left their works, owners of celebrated gardens ve left collections. Ellen Willmott, whose garden at Warley Place, Essex, is now a country park, t drawings she had commissioned of her irises; E. A. Bowles, whose garden at Myddelton House, field, now belongs to the Lea Valley Water Authority, left a mass of papers, including his own wings of *Galanthus* and other genera; the archives of garden designers such as Lanning Roper and ichael Haworth-Booth are also deposited. These gifts and bequests are now safeguarded in rpetuity, and the Lindley Library will continue to provide a safe haven for future gifts and quests, for generations to come.

Brent Elliott
The Royal Horticultural Society

USEFUL ADDRESSES AND TELEPHONE NUMBERS

A

A drawing of *Passiflora laurifolia*, dated 1785,
by Margaret Meen. Reginald Cory bequest, 1936.

A drawing of rudbeckia (probably 1820s)
by James Sowerby. E. A. Bowles bequest, 1954.

B

An early eighteenth-century drawing of tulip 'Prins d'Orange Blanc', attributed to August Sievert (but in 1775 reproduced in C. J. Trew's *Hortus Nitidissimis* as tulip 'Keizer Leopoldus'). Reginald Cory bequest, 1936.

B

A drawing of *Iris cuprea* (now *Iris fulva*) by a Miss Williamson, made in 1905 for Ellen Willmott of Warley Place, Essex. Ellen Willmott bequest, 1935.

C

A coloured stipple engraving after Pierre Antoine Poiteau of a lemon cultivar, 'Limone di ferrari',
from *Histoire Naturelle des Orangers* (1818–22), by Antoine Risso and Poiteau. Reginald Cory bequest, 1936.

C

C

A drawing of *Iris germanica* from 'Flore du Désert', a collection of plant portra[...]
by an anonymous French artist of the early nineteenth century. Reginald Cory bequest, 19[...]

D

A drawing of the blackberry (*Rubus fruticosus*) dated 1784,
by Margaret Meen. Reginald Cory bequest, 1936.

D

D

D

E

E

A coloured engraving of a fig cultivar, 'Fico rubado',
from the *Pomona italiana* (1817–39) of Giorgio Gallesio. Reginald Cory bequest, 1936

E

E

A drawing of the Turkey oak (*Quercus cerris*), probably 1780
by Margaret Meen. Reginald Cory bequest, 193

F

drawing of an iris of the Monspur group, by a Miss Williamson,
made in 1905 for Ellen Willmott of Warley Place, Essex. Ellen Willmott bequest, 1935.

F

F

A drawing of *Prunus hirtipes* 'Semi-plena'
by Winifred Baker. Gertrude Baker bequest, 195?

G

A late seventeenth-century drawing of a form of *Fritillaria meleagris* by Pieter van Holsteyn. Reginald Cory bequest, 1936.

G

G

A late seventeenth-century drawing of cherry cultivars, by Pieter van Holsteyn. Reginald Cory bequest, 1936.

H

H

H

A drawing of daffodil 'Dawn', dated 191[...]
by Edward Augustus Bowles. E. A. Bowles bequest, 195[...]

I

A coloured engraving of *Amaryllis pulverulenta* (now *Hippeastrum striatum*) from *A Selection of Hexandrian Plants* (1831–4) by Mrs Edward Bury (née Priscilla Susan Falkner). Reginald Cory bequest, 1936.

J

J

A drawing of the grape cultivar 'Chasselas verd' by Johann Simon Kerner,
from his *Le Raisin* (1803–8). Kerner produced *Le Raisin* as one of his limited-edition works,
in which all the illustrations were drawn individually rather than printed. Reginald Cory bequest, 1936.

J

A coloured engraving of *Camellia japonica* from the *Flora Japonica* (1835–70) of Franz Philipp von Siebold and J. G. Zuccarini. Reginald Cory bequest, 1936

K

A coloured stipple engraving of *Magnolia × soulangiana* from *Choix des plus belles fleurs* (1827–33)
by Pierre-Joseph Redouté. Reginald Cory bequest, 1936.

K

A drawing of the hawthorn (*Crataegus monogyna*), probably 1780s
by Augusta Smith. Reginald Cory bequest, 1936

L

coloured engraving of *Hydrangea macrophylla* 'Otaksa' from the *Flora Japonica* (1835–70)
Franz Philipp von Siebold and J. G. Zuccarini. Reginald Cory bequest, 1936.

L

L

L

A drawing of *Tropaeolum majus* from 'Flore du Désert', a collection of plant portraits by an anonymous French artist of the early nineteenth century. Reginald Cory bequest, 19

M

A coloured engraving of a sunflower (*Helianthus annuus*)
from *Illustration of the Sexual System of Linnaeus* (1770–77)
by John Miller (Johann Sebastian Müller). Reginald Cory bequest, 1936.

M

M

M

A late eighteenth-century drawing of the common myrtle (*Myrtus communi*
from 'Flora Asiatica', a collection of drawings by anonymous arti
formerly in the collection of the 3rd Earl of Bute. Reginald Cory bequest, 19

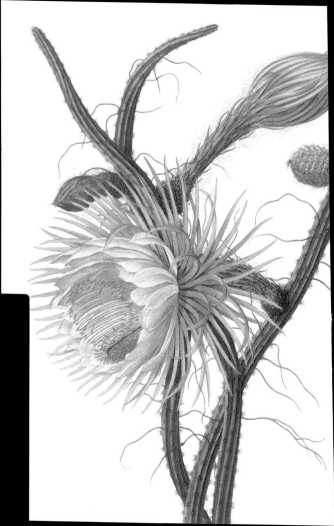

N

coloured engraving after Georg Dionysius Ehret of a night-blooming cereus (*Selenicereus grandiflora*)
m C. J. Trew's *Plantae Selectae* (1750–65). Reginald Cory bequest, 1936.

A drawing of an aconite (probably 182?)
by James Sowerby. E. A. Bowles bequest, 19?

O

An early eighteenth-century drawing on vellum of the vanilla orchid (*Vanilla planifolia*) by Claude Aubriet. Reginald Cory bequest, 1936.

O

O

A drawing of the horse chestnut (*Aesculus × carne*
by Winifred Baker. Gertrude Baker bequest, 19

late eighteenth-century drawing of *Hiptage madablota*, from 'Flora Asiatica', a collection of drawings
by anonymous artists formerly in the collection of the 3rd Earl of Bute. Reginald Cory bequest, 1936.

P Q

A drawing of *Juniperus communis* from 'Flore du Désert', a collection of plant portra
by an anonymous French artist of the early nineteenth century. Reginald Cory bequest, 193

R

coloured engraving of a bouquet of pansies from *Choix des plus belles fleurs* (1827–33)
Pierre-Joseph Redouté. Reginald Cory bequest, 1936.

R

A drawing of the Colorado spruce (*Picea pungens glau*
by Ursula Hodgson. Gift of the artist, 19

S

drawing of the poppy anemone (*Anemone coronaria* var. *phoenicia*)
Edward Augustus Bowles. E.A. Bowles bequest, 1954.

S

S

A drawing of *Wisteria sinensis* (probably 192
by Ruth Collingridge. Reginald Cory bequest, 19

T

coloured engraving after J. Hart of *Helianthemum canescens* (later renamed *H. variabile*), om *Cistineae* (1825–30) by Robert Sweet. Reginald Cory bequest, 1936.

T

U V

U V

u v

A drawing of a snowdrop cultivar, *Galanthus* 'Galate
by Edward Augustus Bowles. E. A. Bowles bequest, 19

W

W

X Y Z

X Y Z